Yes, I Would Marry Him Again

WIVES SALUTE THEIR AFRICAN AMERICAN HUSBANDS

Lori S. Jones Gibbs

Yes Enterprises, LLC
Durham, NC

Yes, I Would Marry Him Again
Wives Salute Their African American Husbands

For bulk discount orders call publisher at 1-888-567-4234
Visit www.yesiwouldmaryyhimagain.com

Publisher Name: Yes Enterprises, LLC.
Publisher Address: 6409 Fayetteville Road Suite 120-141
Publisher City, State: Durham, NC 27713
Publisher Phone: 1-888-567-4234
Publisher Website: www.yesenterprisesllc.com

Library of Congress: 1-521433001

ISBN 13: 978-0-9819749-1-0

Cover Designed by: Linden-Williams Design Studios
Book Designed by: Linden-Williams Design Studios

Disclaimer: All pictures included in this publication have been provided by and printed with the permission of the contributors.

Table of Contents

Foreword

Real Men Real Husbands

Our hearts leapt with joy as my wife, Annette, and I sat listening to our friend Lori Jones Gibbs share with us the premise for the book that you now hold in your hands, *Yes, I Would Marry Him Again.* Many African Americans feel that the images of the Black community in general, and family life in particular, are often portrayed in the media as broken, dysfunctional and without worthy attributes or strengths. While not ignoring the many challenges facing Black families and the relationships between Black men and women, *Yes, I Would Marry Him Again* focuses on the too easily unseen and uncelebrated facts that many African American married couples are still together after many years of marriage, and from their experiences they have much wisdom to offer.

The stories that compose *Yes, I Would Marry Him Again* are the honest reflections of each contributor about her husband and married life. Some of these stories will make you laugh and others will bring you to tears with their compassion and love. The voices of these testimonies are those of women whose relationships with their husbands counter the many negative assumptions and myths about Black men as husbands and fathers. These reflections are romantic, endearing and will endure because they are grounded in the reality of the messiness and majesty that make up the strongest marriages. I met Lori many years ago when she was a young adult active in her church and the community. She has always stood out as a strong, bright and charismatic leader. I am delighted that she has turned her attention and used her gifts to share with the world the insights this book offers.

For over thirty-years I have offered premarital and marital counseling as a Pastor and clinical social worker. This book will contribute greatly to our understanding and the popular discussions about relationships between men and women and married life. People from all walks of life will find this book appealing. Those already married and those who hope to marry someday will find it nothing short of inspiring.

Frederick J. Streets, former Chaplain of Yale University, is the Carl and Dorothy Bennett Professor in Pastoral Counseling, Wurzweiler School of Social Work, Yeshiva University, New York City and Associate Adjunct Professor in Pastoral Theology, Yale University Divinity School. He served for 17 years as the Senior Pastor of the Mount Aery Baptist Church in Bridgeport, CT., and for fifteen years as the Senior Pastor of the Church of Christ in Yale University.

 *"There is no competition in a marriage."*

- K. Gibbs, Sr.

"A man needs to be respected. A woman needs to be loved."

- Sonya T. Catlett

Love

Love is patient, love is kind. It does not envy, it does not boast, it is not proud. It is not rude, it is not self-seeking, it is not easily angered, it keeps no record of wrongs. Love does not delight in evil but rejoices with the truth. It always protects, always trusts, always hopes, always perseveres. Love never fails.

1 Corinthians 13:4-8 NIV

"Three ways to your husband's heart... feed him, favor him and fulfill him."

- Lori Jones Gibbs

Dedication

This book is dedicated to my parents Sarah Claudia Scott and the late Henry Thatchel Jones who were married for 57 years, and my in-laws Fannie Mae and Charlie Gibbs Sr. who celebrated their 58th wedding anniversary on February 12, 2010 for being examples.

To my husband Kenneth D. Gibbs Sr. the inspiration for this book

To all the husbands who embody the teaching of Ephesians 5:25-29 (NKJV): "Husbands, love your wives, just as Christ also loved the church and gave Himself for her, that He might sanctify and cleanse her with the washing of water by the word, that He might present her to Himself a glorious church, not having spot or wrinkle or any such thing, but that she should be holy and without blemish. So husbands ought to love their own wives as their own bodies; he who loves his wife loves himself. For no one ever hated his own flesh, but nourishes and cherishes it, just as the Lord does the church."

To all the wives who are wise enough to embrace the attributes of the virtuous wife described in Proverbs 31:10-31 (NKJV): "Who can find a virtuous wife? For her worth is far above rubies. The heart of her husband safely trusts her; so he will have no lack of gain. She does him good and not evil all the days of her life. She seeks wool and flax, and willingly works with her hands. She is like the merchant ships, she brings her food from afar. She also rises while it is yet night, and provides food for her household, and a portion for her maidservants. She considers a field and buys it; from her profits she plants a vineyard. She girds herself with strength, and strengthens her arms. She perceives that her merchandise is good, and her lamp does not go out by night. She stretches out her hands to the distaff, and her hand holds the spindle. She extends her hand to the poor, yes, she reaches out her hands to the needy. She is not afraid of snow for her household, for all her household is clothed with scarlet. She makes tapestry for herself; her clothing is fine linen and purple. Her husband is known in the gates, when he sits among the elders of the land. She makes linen garments and sells them, and supplies sashes for the merchants. Strength and honor are her clothing; she shall rejoice in time to come. She opens her mouth with wisdom, and on her tongue is the law of kindness. She watches over the ways of her household, and does not eat the bread of idleness. Her children rise up and call her blessed; her husband also, and he praises her: 'Many daughters have done well, but you excel them all.' Charm is deceitful and beauty is passing, but a woman who fears the LORD, she shall be praised. Give her of the fruit of her hands, and let her own works praise her in the gates."

"Success is nothing without someone to share it with."

- From the movie, Lady Sings The Blues

Love and Happiness

Acknowledgements

I thank God, my provider and sustainer, for the life you have given me and the soul mate you sent me to share my life with.

I thank all the wives who shared their salutes and contributed to this book. Your salutes are a testament that African American (Black) marriage is alive and well.

I thank all the husbands profiled in this book for giving your wife a salute to share with the world.

I thank Dr. Frederick (Jerry) Streets for his foreword and allowing an old friend to seek and receive your support. THANK YOU!

I thank editors Kenneth Gibbs and Kenneth Gibbs, Jr.

I thank Claudia Gibbs for your marketing suggestions.

I thank my soror Sonya Harris, for listening and sharing of your time and talents.

I thank Vanessa Nicholas for her creative genius on the graphics and layout of this book.

I thank my children for your encouragement and support. I pray and hope that your dad and I have made you as proud to call us your parents as you have made us proud to be your parents.

"I would marry him again because he loved me unconditionally and would do almost anything in his power to make me happy!"

- Barbara P. Bellinger

Author's Note

I decided to assemble this compilation because of the numerous African American marriages that are working. Though books have been written about fathers and what they mean to daughters, sons and mothers, I have not yet come across a book that served as a tribute to husbands, especially African American husbands. I believe they are the foundation of the family. Why husbands? No matter what other role they may play—father, brother, son and nephew—it is the husband-wife relationship from which solid families are built. I strongly believe that a man who has a relationship with God and a loving, caring, respectful relationship with his mother will know how to love, care for and respect his wife.

I often tell people when talking about my husband, "Yes, I would marry him again!" The various responses I receive amaze me. "Oh that's beautiful." "He must be a special man." "Girl you've got a good one." However the response that has always stayed with me was from a black man who said to me, "I'm glad to hear a black woman speak with such pride, love and respect for her husband. Thank you my sister."

The truth of the matter is, I know there are women out there that feel just as I do when I say "Yes, I would marry him again." These women would be willing to share their stories with others. Unfortunately, we do not verbalize it enough. Some prefer to continue to portray black men in general, and black husbands in particular, as abusive, lazy, absent fathers, cheating husbands, and non-caring good-for-nothing men. However, I know that this is not true. I have been blessed to be married to my husband Kenneth Demire Gibbs, Sr.—a strong example of black manhood—for 30 years. I will share our story with you later.

So what is marriage? For the purpose of this book, marriage is defined as the state of being united to a person of the opposite sex as husband or wife in a consensual, contractual and covenantal relationship recognized by law and in the eyes of God.

I asked each wife to share her perspective on her marriage and husband. How did you meet him? How did you know that he was "the one?" What have been some of your greatest joys together? What storms have you weathered together and how have they made your commitment to your husband stronger? To put it simply, would you marry your husband again and why?

Thus my journey began. I asked myself, "who should I ask to contribute?" Ultimately, I decided to get the stories of everyday women like you and me. Women who've been married a short amount of time (the shortest being eight years), and women who have been married a long time (the longest being over 65 years). Women who have survived the pain of broken relationships, and who have had to look more than once to find "Mr. Right." Women who found love later in life, and women whose beloved husbands are no longer with us. The husbands profiled in this book are not celebrities. They are everyday men. Although not perfect, each strives to follow God and do right by his wife and family. They come from all walks of life—businessmen, lawyers, doctors, clergy, educators, farmers, mechanics, and custodians.

As you read this book be mindful that all the salutes are original and written by wives. These wives all feel a sense of pride and blessings, love, encouragement and support from their husbands. So let the salutes begin!

Lori Jones Gibbs

"My husband loved me...he affectionately called
me his Sa (short for Sarah) - that was his name
for me."

- Sarah C. Jones

"I would marry him again because we both deserve each other's love."

- Denise Gardner

The Salutes

"I married him because I was truly in awe of his relationship with our Creator."

- Cymonda Wilson

We Both Deserve Each Other's Love

Committed

Rodney and Cymonda Wilson

Faithful - Rodney Wilson II

Rodney Wilson II and Cymonda Scrubbs married on May 25, 2002.

We dated for a little over six months before getting engaged. We planned our wedding and were married six months later.

I married Rodney because I was truly in awe of his relationship with our Creator. His faith in God's plan for his life was unlike any other man I had ever dated. Rodney's relationship with God translated into a confidence that no matter the circumstances, things would turn out okay. A lot of folks say that is what they believe, but Rodney truly lives by that principle. Coming in a strong second is laughter. We shared a lot of laughter and spoke for hours when we were getting to know each other. There was always a feeling of easiness whenever I was around him that I found refreshing. Rodney showed sincere interest in my career aspirations and was not intimidated by my professional or personal accomplishments.

There are several reasons why I would marry Rodney again. Rodney loves his family and friends fiercely. It was one of the things I found most attractive about him. He is an amazing father to our two sons, Nafese and Maasai. He is funny, attentive, nurturing and kind. After the birth of our second child, Rodney re-worked his days off so that he could provide care for them every Thursday and Friday. As a result, both children have an extremely close relationship with their father. He is an active participant in their education and takes time to read, practice handwriting and review what Nafese is learning in preschool. With so many women today left to raise a family on their own and without the support of a spouse, I feel blessed to have him as the father of my children.

My husband is also very dedicated to providing service to others. For nearly eight years, Rodney has given his time to feed and uplift the homeless men and women around Auburn Avenue in downtown Atlanta. When the donations ran out, Rodney took a second job to pay for the 125 bag lunches that he prepares himself each week. In 2004, Rodney founded a non-profit organization, Living Unity Thru

Spiritual Ascension, that included a non-denominational church and ministry created to help transition the homeless back into society and the workforce. His hope is to secure a building in the downtown area where he can provide further assistance to those in need.

Our marriage is still in its infancy and has not been without challenges or struggle, but we continue to find the best in one another while working through the rough patches.   He is the right husband for me because he shows me understanding and patience and is constantly striving to be the best person he can be. I thank God for sending Rodney into my life and pray we have many years to come together.

Cymonda Wilson

"I would marry him again because my husband has all of my father's good qualities...generous, hard-working, smart and handsome."

- Edyie Moyer

Melvin and Edyie Moyer

Wet From Head to Toe - Melvin Moyer

Melvin Moyer and Edyie Jo Walker married on October 15, 1988

My father set the bar so high for any man that would be my husband that I knew what qualities to look for at an early age. He told me that I would know if a man really loved me by his actions, and that if I found a man that loved me half as much as he did, I would be blessed.

Well, I met my husband 29 years ago when I was sixteen and he was eighteen. My husband has all of my father's good qualities (generous, hard-working, smart and handsome), and none of his vices (excessive drinking, smoking and womanizing). The first time that I realized that my then boyfriend loved me was when I worked as a cashier at a parking lot, after school, from 3:00-11:00 PM. I only lived two blocks from the parking lot and he lived all the way across town. However, he came to my job every night to take me home. One night he arrived at my job soaking wet from head to toe. When I asked him why he was so wet, he told me that his car would not start, so he ran to meet me. When I told my father the story, he smiled with his eyes. We married on October 15, 1988, seven years later. I married him because he is a wonderful human being with a strong moral compass and an enormous amount of integrity. Like a professional athlete, he continues to hone his skills at being a partner to me so that we maintain a healthy marriage and parenting our three children. Yes, I would most certainly marry him again.

Edyie Moyer

Glover (Sonny) and Denise Gardner

Caramel Skin with Light Brown Eyes
- Glover (Sonny) Gardner

Glover (Sonny) Gardner and Denise Lyman-Pugh married June 16, 1979.

We met in a community college in 1976. I was working part time during the day, and taking evening classes. I had just gone into the registrar's office to cancel my accounting class. Then I saw that his class was right next door to mine. I went right back into the registrar's office and got myself re-registered!

One evening after class, there he stood: a shy stare, nice dimpled smile, big fluffy afro, caramel skin and illuminating light brown eyes. I was mesmerized! He was 26 and I was going to be 19 in March of the following year. I couldn't wait to tell my Aunt Patty about this handsome man at school. I told her that he was real cute, but very 'skinny' (LOL).

I finally built up enough nerve to say 'hello'. He invited me to lunch—it was my first time having a Cherry Coke and eggs "over-easy"! Two years later, we were married and here we are today, 33 years later, the parents of two adult sons who have given us two gorgeous granddaughters.

Over the years, like any marriage, we've had our challenges which have contributed to and strengthened our commitment to each other. Sonny is patient with me and understands me. When all is said and done, just as our wedding dance song stated, "We Both Deserve Each Other's Love."

With all that I know now and what I didn't know then, yes, I'd choose him and yes, I would marry him again.

Denise Gardner

Melvyn and Sylvia Mahon

The Second Time Around - Melyvn V. Mahon

Melvyn V. Mahon and Sylvia L. Brown married December 31, 1994.

I give honor and thanks to God and his son, my Lord and savior Jesus Christ, for his many blessings, tender mercies and bringing Melvyn into my life.

There was a time when I feasted with my eyes looking only for a tall, dark, handsome, and muscular man. Sadly, those men usually broke my heart, killed my self-esteem, and the relationships ended in disaster. My ex-boyfriend had his best friend burn down my condo, and with it all that was dear and precious to me. All that I had left was my purse and the clothes I had on my back. He lived by that old saying, "if I can't have you nobody will!" I was glad to get out of that relationship with my life and sanity. That was a very dark time in my life and I asked God to have His will in my life. I trusted, prayed, and believed.

God sent me Melvyn, an interventional cardiologist, who was a divorced father raising two children. He was and still is a dedicated, loving and absolutely wonderful man. First was the friendship that flourished out of disaster. Over the next four years, we dated wanting to make sure that our relationship was real and would stand the test of time. We married just short of a five year courtship.

I have never met anyone like Mel nor will I ever again. He is brilliant, honest, loving, driven, truly loves his family, and generous (to a fault at times). He is a wonderful provider, my lover and best friend. We have been blessed with one child together and two from his previous marriage. We've been together twenty years (with fifteen years of wedded bliss) and hopefully we'll have many more together.

I love him more and more each day and wouldn't hesitate to marry him again. We have had our share of good times and bad times, tests and trials. Despite the challenges, including those that come with life in today's economy, we are still together—stronger and more in love than ever before. I can truly say that when you follow your heart, trust that inner voice and ask God for guidance, you will find that special someone who is meant just for you.

Sylvia B. Mahon

James (Jim) and Marcia Griffin

My Partner and Blessing - James (Jim) Griffin

James (Jim) Griffin and Marcia Johnson married December 17, 1975

Jim and I first met when I was a senior at Fisk University. I had gone to the university's career planning center to confirm my job offer with Xerox. Jim was there recruiting for the University of Pennsylvania's Wharton School of Business MBA program. He and I began to converse and I told him of my plans to start my professional career with Xerox. He suggested that I postpone starting my career and instead pursue my MBA at UPENN. You guessed it - I applied and was accepted. However, I did not receive a scholarship. So there I was with no job (because I had notified Xerox of my change in plans and thus turned down the job offer) and no funding to attend graduate school at Wharton. I told Jim if he is going to recruit he needs to make sure he has a financial package for his recruits. After that encounter, Jim had the audacity to ask me out on a date! I don't know why but I decided I go out with him.

We dated for four years and were married in Tanzania, Africa (where my parents lived) in a beautiful yet quaint wedding ceremony attended by my parents and a few of my fathers co-workers. When we returned to the United States, my now in-laws held a reception in our honor in Lakeland, Florida which was attended by family and friends.

Jim is my very best friend. He is a great person and is blessed with a kind spirit and pure brilliance. Jim is a man who sacrifices for his family. We are the parents of four adult children (two boys and two girls), and Jim has always put our needs before his own. He's always been there whenever we needed him in any way. My parents say that he's a **GREAT** son-in-law, and have been delighted that he joined our family.

Jim is also a man who sacrifices for others, and seeks opportunities to help others realize their dreams as well. In 1995 with Jim's encouragement, financial and moral support we founded HomeFree-USA, a non-profit organization to help people achieve the dream of homeownership safely, securely and with peace of mind.

Jim is my partner and a blessing to me. He is dependable, handsome, loving, genuine, caring and a provider. He is the reason I tell the unmarried, "Marry your best friend. Someone you can laugh with all the time and you know has your back!" Jim is a strong, self-assured and hardworking black man. We have been married for 35 wonderful years and yes, I would be honored, happy and proud to marry Jim Griffin again!

By Marcia J. Griffin

"After an encounter he had the audacity to ask me out on a date...I've been blessed ever since."

- Marcia Griffin

"Love is moral even without legal marriage, but marriage is immoral without love."

- Anonymous

God's Favor

Share My Love

Fredrick and Judith Davis

His Love for Me Is Modeled After His Love for God
- Fredrick Amos Davis

Fredrick Amos Davis and Judith Anita Hayes married August 18, 1979

This man makes me laugh and I've realized that the combination of laughter and love makes marriage work. Why would I marry this man again? In the words of my husband, "I thought you would never ask".

"This man" is Fredrick Amos Davis. I remember when I first heard his name. He was 16-years-old and I was 15. In February of 1973 the question on every girl's mind at Saint Thomas Aquinas High School was, "who are you inviting to the Sadie Hawkins dance in March?" I really gave it little thought in February but as March approached I was confident that the boy I had in mind to invite would accept my invitation. Much to my chagrin, he did not accept my invite because he was going to the dance with another girl—a girl who didn't even attend St. Thomas! Fredrick Amos Davis' name was given to me by my girlfriends who attended high school with him. They previously informed me that Fredrick liked me. Well I was "desperate" and was not going to be out done, so I made "the call". He answered the phone and I began telling him the reason for my call and my request. So on March 8, 1973 at St. Thomas Aquinas high school in Fort Lauderdale, Florida, Fredrick became my boyfriend. Little did I know on August 18, 1979, six years later he would become my husband and 31 years later I can unequivocally declare I would marry this man again!

Fredrick Amos Davis, born in Florida to the late John Henry Davis and Julia Hannah Davis, was the answer to a 15-year-old girl's prayer request. In 1973, I began to mention in my nightly prayers to God what I desired in a boyfriend. That prayer—which I can clearly recall some 36 years later—was that God would send me a Christian boyfriend. I believed that if God sent me someone who really loved the Lord, then I could truly love him. Now I was only praying for a 'boyfriend' not a husband (I was only 15). But I can truly say that God in his loving kindness sent me a boyfriend that later became my husband. I would marry Fredrick again because his love for me is modeled after his love for God. Fredrick Amos Davis, also known as Dr. Love, loves his God, his wife, his sons and his family. He is learning the mystery of loving this woman and cherishing and parenting our three sons into men. I would marry Fredrick Amos Davis again and again and again without a doubt because I know that he is a man after my heart and I believe also after God's.

Judith Anita Davis

Davis Family

"During my darkest moments, he stood by me and lovingly showed me what it means to nurture and love."

- Lynn Richardson

Demietrius and Lynn Richardson

Prayer Answered – Demietrius Richardson

Demietrius Richardson and Lynn Hameen married March 4, 1995

In my early twenties, I prayed for a man who was God-fearing, honest, hard working and who had a good relationship with his mother. God blessed me with Demietrius. We started dating in December of 1993, were engaged four months later in March of 1994, and were married one year later in March of 1995. Fifteen years later, I still feel like a newlywed! Demietrius has been my best friend and biggest cheerleader. My mother and grandmother loved him from day one—sometimes I think they like him more than they like me! He's just that kind of special person.

As I have risen to the top of my career professionally and financially, he has never shown even a hint of insecurity or jealousy, and has always seen our union as a partnership. Sometimes that meant he worked while I rested and other times it meant I worked while he pursued his own business and took care of the kids. Cooking, cleaning, making baby formula and combing hair for our three daughters: you name it, Demietrius has done it – and happily, I should add. When I traveled several times a week while I was a corporate vice president of a major financial institution, my sweetie would have my luggage packed when I had to leave for the airport at 4am and he would have my dinner and bath prepared when I returned home at 10pm after a long cross-country day trip. The next morning, the cycle would repeat itself and he would be right there with bags, vitamins and breakfast waiting for me to hit the runway again.

During my darkest moments, Demietrius stood by me and lovingly showed me, in the very nature of Christ, what it means to nurture and love "through good times and bad times." Even when I've made mistakes, I can't remember a time when he made me feel anything less than hopeful about looking up, getting up, and doing it better next time.

I love Demietrius. He was sent to me as a gift from God. I am very thankful to have a man in my life who loves God and is growing with me spiritually in his walk as a Deacon and in my walk as a minister. My life transformation over the past 17 years has been motivated by my desire to be a better person so I can be as good to Demietrius as he has been to me. When you see a person like me—successful, young, happy, anointed, and living her dreams at the top of her career—know that it is by the grace of God. For me, that grace has manifested in the person of my lover, my friend, my soulmate: Demietrius Richardson. Without a doubt, I would marry him again.

Lynn Richardson

"Although I couldn't believe it - I said yes to a man who only months ago was a stranger."

- Juanita Montgomery

Kevin and Juanita Montgomery

God Sent – Kevin G. Montgomery

Kevin G. Montgomery and Juanita Cooper married: June 18, 1983

Kevin and I dated 4 1/2 months before we got married.

I married Kevin because I knew without a doubt that he was the person God had sent to be my husband. When we met in Bible Institute, January 18, 1983, he asked me to go with him to a basketball game. Not knowing him at all, I told him that I was busy that night and would not be able to go. Instead of giving up, he asked if it was OK to give me his telephone number. When I said, "OK," he gave me his business card with his personal phone number on the back. He then said, "while you are standing there, you could give me yours." I was hesitant at first but I wanted him to know he wasn't the only one with a business card! So I pulled out my business card and wrote my number on the back just like he did. He was persistent and asked a favor of me the next night—to take his cousin home from church. I was amazed that he was related to this young lady whom I had known all of her life! That evening he called me to thank me for taking his cousin home and we got into deep family conversation, finding out that I knew his grandmother, aunts and cousins but never knew him. We have been talking ever since. When he asked me to marry him on March 3, 1983. I didn't say yes right away—it took me three days. Although I couldn't believe it—saying yes to a man who only months ago had been a stranger—I knew it was right.

I would marry Kevin again and again because he is truly a man after God's own heart and I believe he loves and is in love with me. He is a loving and caring husband and the best father to our three children Shaniqua, Kevin II & Charita. Kevin, I love you!

Juanita Montgomery

Bishop Harold I. Williams and Pastor Shirley Caesar

A Praying Man - Bishop Harold Ivory Williams

Bishop Harold I. Williams and Pastor Shirley Caesar married June 26, 1983

During my twenties and thirties I had the opportunity to meet several eligible Christian bachelors and I had more marriage proposals than I can remember. To be honest I was so preoccupied with my career and ministry I just didn't have time to develop a relationship.

I had known Bishop Harold Ivory Williams pretty much all of my life. Even though he lived in Baltimore, Maryland he traveled quite extensively and his travels would bring him to the Raleigh/Durham area. It was during his travel to Durham in January of 1983, at White Rock Baptist Church during the Annual Citywide Revival that I, along with members of all the Mount Calvary Holy Churches of America in North Carolina, was there to support our Bishop. As members of Mount Calvary Holy Churches of America, we saw this as a great honor, not only for him to be the keynote speaker, but for the entire Mount Calvary Holy Churches of America. History was made during this time as Bishop Harold Ivory Williams was the first Pentecostal preacher ever to preach in the City Wide Revival, so you can imagine how excited we were.

I was in attendance each night, and someone said to me "I think he likes you." Of course I did not believe it and yet on Saturday morning he invited me to brunch. After we finished brunch he immediately left and returned to Baltimore. For the next two weeks Bishop Williams called me several times a day. Finally, he made the call that caused my life to change forever! I had received many proposals from Bishops, Pastors, Singers and Deacons, but there was something about his proposal that let me know "This is my lifetime partner." When he asked for my hand in marriage, I said, "Come to Durham and ask me." He did not come empty handed, he came with a beautiful diamond ring. He asked, and I immediately said "YES!" However, I reminded him that from the time I was 12-years-old I had been taking care of my mother and this would continue until one of us changes time for eternity. He quickly replied,

"I will do anything to help you take care of Mother Caesar."

Five months later, we were married in an incredible ceremony held at Durham High School Auditorium. During the wedding ceremony we had more people outside the auditorium than inside. There were 106 wedding participants, which included a miniature bride and groom, three best men and three maids of honor - some say it was the largest wedding to take place in the State of North Carolina at that time!

Yes! I did marry a wonderful man, a man filled with wisdom who believes that Jesus plus education equals success. Bishop Williams believes in education to the extent that at the age of fifty he earned his GED, and went on to earn a bachelor degree, a Masters degree and two PhDs. I call that a phenomenal man. The qualities that drew me to him most are that he's a praying man that is kindhearted, has a giving spirit, loves the Lord and I am very sure that he loves me. My husband is also a very supportive and attentive man that has always taken care of me and encouraged me to pursue my professional endeavors of singing, traveling and my ministry.

We celebrated twenty eight wonderful years of a blessed marriage this year. Yes, I would marry him again. I know this man and I love this man—a strong man, a loving man, a caring man and a giving man. That's my husband Bishop Harold Ivory Williams. In twenty two years we can do it again at our Golden (50th) Wedding Anniversary. Thank You Bishop Williams for the opportunity to be your wife.

Pastor Shirley Caesar Williams

"I know where I've been with this man - only God knows where we're going."

- Pastor Shirley Caesar Williams

*"It does not matter what the future brings, I am
sure that we will spend it together."*

- Frances Dyer Stewart

Emotionally Yours

You and I

James (Jim) and Frances Dyer Stewart

Third Time is the Charm - James (Jim) Stewart

James A. "Jim" Stewart and Frances Dyer married on February 17, 1990

We dated for 3 ½ years and were on the outs when Lori Gibbs decided to throw a surprise birthday party for her husband, Ken, in October 1989. Lori, knowing that we were on the outs, decided to invite us separately to the party. I was incensed. I thought Lori was my friend and could not understand how she could extend an invitation to Jim—a man she barely knew and only through me. I was planning to invite another guy until she advised me that she had invited Jim. What was I to do but contact Jim (through an intermediary) and suggest that we go to the party together to avoid an embarrassing situation, me with my date and him with whomever. Although I was still smitten by Jim, I was looking for a firm commitment. He had enjoyed "the milk" for almost four years and I had shut off the spigot. The ultimatum was unspoken: take the package or move on. I had planned to use the party as a new beginning for me with someone new. Needless to say, that party was the beginning of a new committed phase in our relationship.

We later shared Thanksgiving and Christmas with our families as a couple. Then on January 13th we traveled to Lake Tahoe for skiing. We had been looking for housing to share together (neither of us was anxious for marriage as we each had two divorces under our belts). It was during this trip that Jim informed me that we could not live together in our town without the benefit of marriage—his mom would not hear of it. I could have cared less, I was a modern woman! Apparently, it was OK to spend each and every evening together, keep clothes and toiletries at the other's residence, and sleep over—but not buy a house together unless we were married. Was this a proposal, I wanted to know. "What do you think?" was the answer. We married six weeks later in a quiet, private ceremony with our parents and relatives, in the home of Jim's sister, my friend, who had introduced me to Jim four years earlier. Interestingly enough Jim's mom and my aunt had tried to introduce us (prior to the 2nd marriages) 6 years earlier!
I married Jim because he is the most warm, kind and decent person

that I have ever met. He is calm and giving, I am fiery and crazy. It was not my intention to marry anyone ever again. This is our third marriage each, but you know what they say, "third time is a charm." He is so special that I was willing to ignore my sacred rule of no men with kids—Jim had a son who has become my only and wonderful son.

Yes, I would MARRY JIM STEWART AGAIN AND AGAIN AND AGAIN. I have spent the past 20 years in bliss and continue to this day. My life is ABSOLUTELY WONDERFUL and I would not trade one thing. I have his commitment and love, which is the greatest gift of all, and I gladly return to him. Jim Stewart is the love of my life, my best friend and confidant. It does not matter what the future brings, I am sure that we will spend it together. If not, I am better for this journey.

Frances Dyer Stewart

"I love him because every time I look at him, I fall in love all over again."

- Gwen Walker McCorvey

William and Gwen McCorvey

Just Because- William McCorvey

William McCorvey and Gwen Walker married August 12, 1995

We met January 1, 1987 and dated off-and-on for eight years.

I married William and would marry him again:

Because we love each other unconditionally.

Because he is my soul mate.

Because he cares about me and understands my feelings.

Because he listens to my worries and helps me through them.

Because he's patient with me and doesn't try to manipulate me into someone I'm not.

Because we're very compatible despite our different personalities—he's reserved and I'm outgoing.

Because he knows how to give every day—not just on special occasions or when it's easy or convenient.

Because he makes time for me regardless of his busy and hectic schedule.

Because he lets me know that I matter.

Because he is a loving son, father and grandfather who cares about his family.

Because we enjoy laughing and humorously teasing each other all the time.

Because he shows his love for me in every way that matters.

Because we enjoy being together, whether we're playing board games, cards, watching TV, golfing, vacationing or just cuddling.

Because he's an intelligent, well educated and hard working man.

Because we give each other space to learn and grow.

Because he is a spiritual and religious man who loves the Lord.

Because he is an honest, fair and compassionate man.

Because he makes me feel good about myself, even when I'm not at my best.

Because he is my best friend and I would trust him with my life.

Because every time I look at him I fall in love all over again.

Because we both brought the better parts of ourselves to our marriage.

Because he is a tall, dark and handsome man who is just as appealing to me today as he was the first time we met.

Because we kiss and express our love to each other daily.

Because we enjoy our children and grandchildren whenever we're all together.

Because I couldn't imagine my life without him.

Because we both know the power of prayer.

Because he assisted me with the care of my mother who resided with us for four years.

Because our marriage, which spans fifteen years, is a testament of love, faith, respect and happiness.

Because he inspires me to reach greater heights.

Because he trusts me to manage our personal finances.

Because we can talk to each other about anything.

Because when we argue, it's with love.

Because we have been each other's source of support, comfort, love and friendship.

Because our marriage is a gift from God that He Himself designed.

Because with William in my life, I am living the life that I imagined...a dream come true!

Gwen Walker McCorvey

McCorvey Grandchildren

Dwayne (Kenny) and Kara Turner

The Gentle Giant - Dwayne (Kenny) Turner

Dwayne (Kenny) Turner and Kara Vample married October-26-2002

My husband is a gentle giant that could be mistaken for a pit bull so do not cross him because you will definitely feel his wrath. He is a protector yet not overbearing, sensitive yet strong, confident yet modest, candid yet compassionate and loves his family beyond measure.

I knew he was a keeper but the deal was sealed for me while visiting him once in Portugal. First of all I was so impressed with how he had immersed himself in their culture. One day he had me try a strawberry tart of some sort and it quickly became one of my favorites. We were out at the mall one evening and I (of course, trying to be cute) had declined his offer for some of the tarts earlier in the day. As the shops were closing I decided to tell him that I wanted some of the tarts. Speaking in Portuguese, he called a bakery that was close to the mall and asked if they could stay open until he got there. He then ran down the street in the pouring rain to get me some of my favorite deserts, and he did so without any complaints.

He is that same man today and the reason why I love him so. There is nothing that he would not do for his family or his friends. He is a very loving and devoted husband and father and at the end of the day (when I'm angry at him for who knows what this time) this is what gives me peace. I know if God called me to leave this earth today, our daughters will be in good hands.

There are no "ifs," "ands," or "buts" about it, I would definitely marry him again. It is my special prayer that our girls will grow up and share their lives with someone just like their "Daddy."

I love you, Kenny.

By Kara Vample Turner

Daniel and Juanita Massenburg

The Encourager - Daniel (Danny) Massenburg

Daniel Massenburg and Juanita Blackwell married July 17, 1976

Thirty-six years ago, a very energetic, dashing, handsome and extremely smart young man approached me and expressed a strong interest in spending quality time together. This young man had already completed both a Bachelor's and Master's Degree from North Carolina Central University, and was employed as a Police Officer with the City of Durham Police Department. Although Daniel Massenburg was gainfully employed and I was just a sophomore attending North Carolina Central University, our relationship blossomed into a wonderful romance. After two years of a whirlwind adventure of fun, laughter and romance and after my graduation, we were married on Saturday, July 17, 1976 at 3:00pm. After 34 glorious years, I'm proud to say that we've remained together!

Daniel "Danny" Massenburg has been a strong supporter of all of my dreams and aspirations and continues to encourage my growth and elevation. He is my friend, my lover, and my confidant, and he has been a loving husband and fantastic father to our daughter, Mundi Massenburg. One of the things I cherish most is the time we spend worshipping, and praying together when we attend church as a family. He is an extremely loving man who I love with all my heart. When it is all said and done, I would definitely marry Daniel Massenburg all over again.

-Juanita Blackwell Massenburg

Juanita Massenburg and daughter Mundi

Rudolph and Glenda Gabriel

Home Run Hero - Rudolph Gabriel

Rudolph Gabriel and Glenda Galbert married September 6, 1975

Our story started as a boy and girl on the softball field.

The ball goes high into the air and nobody catches it. In fact, the ball is kicked so far that the outfielders have to run after it, but it evades them. I fly past first base, and swish past second—I am one with the wind. As I round third base, I hear him yelling, "You can do it." I head for home plate, giving my all to win it for him. After all, he had not hesitated to choose me first when picking his team. I accelerate my speed and in a flash I cross home base, safe. Cheers erupted all around and I received a round of high-fives—but none more precious than his for he is my hero.

Flash forward, we ended up attending every single school together. Even though we did not date, when my mom asked me who I would like to attend my special 16th birthday dinner, I did not hesitate to choose him—my hero and friend. Through the years we talked casually and infrequently, but when we did chat the conversations were like a gentle breeze—soft, easy and fragrant. He always made me laugh and smile with something witty and smart to say—even though I was shy and given to be serious (some even said unapproachable).

On one special evening, I went to a political discussion on my college campus. He was active in college politics, the editor of the student body newspaper, and was there at the meeting. Although I noticed that this boy was now a very nice looking young man, I had other things to do—like reading "Their Eyes Were Watching God". Thankfully, he noticed me and made his way across the room. He calculated that the proper place to start our conversation was about the book, and he was right. One thing lead to another and he asked me if I would like to get a bite to eat after the meeting. Surprising myself, I said yes and the conversations went from infrequent to late night, every day, must-have talks.

I discovered that he is the one and he had always been the one. Six months later, swish goes the wedding dress as I walk down the aisle to meet my prince. He has never been more handsome, more dashing and more mine, standing before God and others, to say "I do." In his eyes is the promise of true love, strength of character, and, yes girls, plain old desire. In his eyes I saw that I was the one and had always been the one for him.

Nearly thirty-five years later, he is still that prince in shining armor. He is delicious in his thirst for life, warmth, wit, intelligence, and a generous heart. My heart still goes swish every time our eyes meet, we are wrapped in each other's warm embrace and share a kiss. My heart still goes swish when he calls my name, gentle like the breeze, just like when we were kids, with the same wonder and promise. My heart still goes swish when I touch his hands—feeling loved, safe, and secure, just like when I scored that home run. By God's grace I have been given the man of my dreams, and I most certainly would marry him again!

Glenda Gabriel

"In him I found a man and a great partner."

- Juanita B. Massenburg

"Yes, I would marry him again and have already done so!"

- Fannie M. Gibbs

Always and Forever

Spend My Life with You

Charlie and Fannie Mae Gibbs

The Provider – Charlie (Charles) Gibbs Sr.

Charlie Gibbs Sr. and Fannie Mae Long married February 2, 1952

Although we both lived in Sanford, Florida I met Charles on a farm in Fairport, New York. He delivered ice and I found him to be very attractive. We dated for three years and then married. Prior to meeting Charles, I had a son. When I shared that news with him, he simply said "as my wife, your son is my son." I can honestly say that he has always treated my son as though he was his natural born child, just as he treated the five children we had together.

To our surprise both our fathers knew each other prior to our meeting. They both lived and worked in Sanford. It wasn't until Charles came to my parents home to pick me up for a date that I found this out. My father said he worked with a Gibbs and that boy (Charles) must be his son because he looks just like him.

Yes, I would marry Charles again and have already done so: Charles and I renewed our vows in 1986. This recommitment was important to us. I was twenty-years-old and he was twenty-seven when we first married, and we wanted to reaffirm our love and commitment to each other as Christians. During the first fourteen years of our marriage, I had already given my life to God and prayed that my husband would do the same. When he did, we wanted to reaffirm our love and commitment to each other as Christians.

Although he is now retired, Charles is a thoughtful, hard working family man who has always provided for and protected our family. When Charles would come home from work the very first questions he would ask are "how are you feeling?" and "where are the children?" In all honesty, Charles would sometimes annoy me with his constant inquiry of wanting to know where our children were when he came home from work. As the children got older he persisted and insisted on knowing their whereabouts.

Like any marriage we have had our ups and downs yet it has been a good marriage and worth sticking together. Now that we are in our golden years, our marriage has changed but is still strong. Although wiser we are dealing with some of the issues that come with old age such as Charles hearing not being as strong as it use to be. We have gotten used to being home together twenty-four hours a day, seven days a week. We go to church together and despite living on a fixed income of retirement pension and social security, Charles is still providing for the two of us.

Our marriage has truly been one "for better or for worse" and Charles has made sure we had a lot more better than worse. For that and many other reasons I love him and would marry him for a third time.

Fannie Mae Gibbs

"I would marry him again because he has the qualities most women look for in a man. He's God-conscious, handsome, loving, caring, kind-hearted and funny."

- Pamela S. Jones

Lyle and Pamela Jones

Committed - Lyle (Hassan) Jones

Lyle Jones and Pamela Slocum married: October 28,1978

We dated approximately eight years prior to marriage. We were high school sweethearts, then became teenagers in love. At the age of seventeen and eighteen we became teen parents of two boys. During my pregnancy with our second child, my future husband, at the age of eighteen, took a responsible approach and found an apartment for us to live in. We were a family of four, living basically as a married couple. While sharing an apartment together, we had our fair share of issues and difficult situations just like most couples. Despite these problems, my future husband was still committed to his family, by providing for and taking care of us. After a few years of living together I finally married my handsome, loving, caring husband.

I would marry my husband over and over again. Why? Because he's my best friend, my soulmate and has been for forty years. We now have three sons Lyle Jr., Lonnie and Leneil. From their loins have come our ten grandchildren. During the course of our forty years together my husband has always been a committed family man, who gave love and support to his wife and children. Now that our children are grown, he gives that same love and support to our grandchildren. My husband is a very busy man, but one thing I can say for sure, he takes time out for me. We vacation twice a year, dine out, take walks, or sometimes simply sit at home and listen to a little mellow music or watch a video. We laugh a lot—my husband's a funny guy and has a great sense of humor. He also sends me flowers every so often (just because), with an "I love you card" attached. Most importantly he's a man of God, which enables him to live accordingly. With that being said my husband has the qualities most women look for in a man. He's God-conscious, handsome, loving, caring, kindhearted and funny. I love him unconditionally. My husband is one in a million and I would be honored to marry him again.

Pamela Jones

Thomas C. (T.C.) and Stella Adams

My Valentine - Thomas C. (T.C.) Adams III

Thomas C. (T.C.) Adams III and Stella Jones married July 4, 1982

My husband T. C. and I met when he hitched a ride with me and his fraternity (frat) brother to DC to spend time. It was snowing and I did not want to drive to DC alone. I enjoyed his company and we became fast friends.

A few months later, just after Valentine's Day, he came by the restaurant where I worked and asked me how my Valentine's Day went. I shared with him that I had received a homemade card and a 25¢ hamburger special from McDonald's—not exactly the greatest Valentine's Day possible. T.C. looked pained, and began to share with me that if I had been his Valentine, I would have received a dozen beautiful red roses, a delicious dinner AND A MOVIE. Oh man, like I really needed to hear that! I secretly vowed I would spend next Valentine's Day with him and I did.

Our first date didn't occur for another two months, when the Alpha's on my campus were having their annual Black and Gold Ball. Well, all of my friends wanted to know which Alpha was taking me to the ball: T.C. or his frat brother? (They could see what I had not—that I was actually spending more time hanging out with T.C. and his frat brother than I was with his frat brother alone). I told them whoever asked me first.

Unbeknownst to me, T.C. asked his frat brother what his relationship with me was exactly and was told we were "just friends." So T.C. asked him for permission to take me to the Black and Gold ball and apparently it was granted. Lucky me!! We had the best date EVER and he was true to his gentlemanly word: there were flowers, dinner and dancing. I felt like I was on a cloud! From that day to this I have been his and his alone.

T. C. and I fell in love the summer of 1982 working to elect H. M. "Mickey" Michaux to Congress from the 2nd Congressional District.

This would be the first of many campaigns we would work together. There were four couples that ended up getting married because they worked together on that (ultimately unsuccessful) campaign - maybe we should have concentrated more on the campaign. T. C. asked me to marry him during the lull between the 1st and 2nd Primary. We eloped to Dillon, SC and were married on the 4th of July. We like to say that there are always fireworks in our marriage and especially when we celebrate our anniversary.

When we married I promised him children who would tug at his knees when he got home shouting "Daddy! Daddy!" T. C. turned out to be a wonderful father to our three gorgeous and brilliant children: Thomas who attends Howard University School of Law, Danielle, a newly elected politician and William our youngest, who attends North Carolina Central University. He taught our sons to be strong intelligent black men and our daughter to be a lady with high standards and high expectations. He taught our children to love the LORD, to be proud of their heritage and to embrace learning. He is a good father.

I truly love him because he utterly and completely loves me just as I am - no make-up, two braids (Cynthia McKinney style), jeans and a t-shirt. He is the most brilliant man I know, and he is a pretty Black man to boot. My husband is ARROGANT and I love that about him. My husband is old world courtly and a gentleman of the first order. He remains my best friend on the planet. We can spend hours and hours lost in our own company contemplating the latest conspiracy theories, the intricacies of quantum mechanics, and how the big bang theory and other theories of the universe confirm the existence of our omniscient and omnipresent GOD. Yes, we are that nerdy and proud of it!

Twenty-eight years and three gorgeous and brilliant children later, I am happy and complete because he is part of my life. I cannot imagine a multi-verse where we are not together; such a world would have to be without comfort, without joy, and without love.

By Stella Adams

"My husband is old world courtly and a gentleman of the first order."

- Stella Adams

Robert (Bobby) and LaTasha Gaddy

Like His Father – Robert (Bobby) E. Gaddy, Jr.

Robert (Bobby) E. Gaddy, Jr. and LaTasha Best married June 8, 2002

It was a hot and sunny day when we met at a North Carolina Central University football game. He was working as an off duty police officer and I was working part-time with the ticket office. We had a few joking words and exchanged contact information before the end of the game. I still remember how he looked in the uniform and thinking that I had not previously dated a man who carries a gun and has arresting powers for a career. I was reluctant to date him because he was a police officer and the risk involved with a law enforcement career. However, I knew he was my future mate when I took him home to meet my parents for Sunday service and dinner. He proposed in 2002, at the Omega Psi Phi Mardi Gras—a special evening because I was inducted as an official member of Delta Sigma Theta Sorority. We were married in a small chapel in Myrtle Beach, South Carolina with only immediate family there to celebrate our union.

Most people would tell you to watch how a man treats his mother and that is an indication of how he will treat his wife. I would disagree. I think you should evaluate the relationship of the man with his father and that is an indication of what type of man he will be in his own household. I have never had the opportunity to meet my husband's father because he died before we met (while my husband was in college). However, I feel that I know him and the type of father he was to his family. My husband and his family have shared so many stories about what his father taught him and how he managed the household. What I know of their relationship makes me proud to have married Bobby. I know his father would be proud of the man he has become. My husband is a gentleman in every meaning of the word. He has so many wonderful qualities. He is a protector who models integrity, faithfulness, love, and patience. He's affectionate, chivalrous, fun and compassionate.

As in most marriages, we have had our share of ups and downs. Through it all, my husband has been the steady rock that has held us together and kept us moving in a positive direction. We currently have two children, Isaiah and Kymberly. Our daughter was diagnosed with a genetic metabolic condition when she was six months old, and we did not know if she would live. God has blessed us not only to be able to manage and maintain her quality of life but we have gained the patience of Job and the strength and courage of David. It was Bobby who kept my spirits high and encouraged me to remain steadfast.

Since marriage, Bobby has been my consistent rock and I have been able to lean on him—especially during the illness of our daughter, Kymberly. During this most difficult time, he showed me how having a wonderful mate is essential to the marriage. I love Bobby unconditionally. He is not only an exceptional husband, but is also a devoted father, son, brother, uncle, and police officer. I write this tribute to show that I not only love my lifetime helpmate, but I appreciate his devotion, love and dedication. I love him now, forever and always. Yes, I would say, "I DO" again.

LaTasha Best Gaddy

Gaddy Family

"I knew he was my future mate when I took him home to meet my parents for Sunday service and dinner."

- LaTasha Best Gaddy

Marvin and Candace Spann

The First Time Ever I Saw Your Face - Marvin Spann

Marvin Spann and Candace Thornton married June 20, 1998

My husband and I met at UCLA. I was actually in love with him long before we met. The first night I saw him was the night before my freshman year started. As soon as I laid eyes on him, I told everyone I was with, "Look! There's my husband." Of course I didn't know his name or anything about him, but it was as if I recognized him. From that point on, I always referred to him as my future husband. We were both pre-med students and had a lot of mutual friends, so we traveled in the same circles. However, it took two long years before he finally kissed me (and only after being tipped off by a mutual friend about my feelings). From that point on, we have been inseparable. After graduating from college, we attended Meharry Medical College together. During medical school, he was my study partner, my support system, and my best friend. There was a time during our first year that I doubted myself. I remember those nights, asking myself if I was really cut out to be a doctor. He made me believe in myself again and helped me realize that I was just as capable as anyone else there. We were married after our second year of medical school.

After graduating from medical school, we moved to New York City for our residencies—his in general surgery and mine in dermatology. During a time that would have been stressful for any couple, we were blissfully happy. Despite the lack of sleep and long hours, he always found time to be with me and found ways to let me know how important I was to him. He has always been the type to be happier on the sofa snuggling than out at clubs or on the street. He has also always been so funny. It is amazing that in the middle of New York City, the most fun and enjoyable place to be was at home with him.

Our daughter was born three years after we moved to New York and our son was born 21 months later. He is a wonderful father. He is very warm and affectionate with the children. He is a firm disciplinarian, but the children always know that he loves them more than anything. He can't stand for any of us to be upset with him. Under his tough exterior is a pile of mush when it comes to his family. There was a time when our daughter was five that she got mad at him. She was so angry that she was in tears. He drew her a bath and filled the bathtub with rose petals. She took one look at it and yelled with a big smile on her face, "Daddy, I'm not mad at you anymore!"

I realize every day how lucky I am to share my life with this man. After he completed his general surgery training, he completed a fellowship in Plastic Surgery at the University of Utah. We moved to Las Vegas (my hometown) about a year-and-a-half ago. I now have the pleasure of sharing my personal and my professional life with him, as we work together also. As I write this, I am thinking back to the first time I saw him nearly 18 years ago. I realize now that I did recognize him. He was, and still is, the man of my dreams.

By Candace Thornton Spann

"As soon as I laid eyes on him, I told everyone I was with, "Look! There's my husband."

- Candace Thornton Spann

"Little did I know that my decision to attend North Carolina College would transform my life forever."

- Deloris B. Harris

Because You Loved Me

Gone But Not Forgotten

Charles and Deloris Harris

Irreplaceable - Charles Edward Harris

Charles Harris and Deloris Bradley married June 12, 1971

We were married at St. John African Methodist Episcopal Church in Marion, SC. I spent all of my formative years in Marion, SC—from birth until graduation from high school, at 16 years old. During my senior year of high school, I had the arduous task of deciding on a college to attend. My favorite math teacher was taking graduate courses during the summers at North Carolina College (NCC) and suggested that I consider going there. I had never heard of the college, but based on the advice of my highly respected teacher, I decided to apply and was accepted. I then made the decision to matriculate at this college located in the north state.

Little did I know that my decision to attend NCC would transform my life forever more. Not only did I get a BS Degree in math, but during the fall of my senior year (1968), I met the love of my life, my best friend, my soul mate – Charles Edward Harris. I think we were destined to get together because I met him briefly the summer prior to meeting him in the fall. At that time, he basically shrugged me off after being introduced by a mutual friend. A different mutual friend took me to his apartment for a party and this time he saw me in a different and much more favorable light. I knew that he was extremely special and my emotions had been touched—so much so, that we started dating during my senior year. In total, we dated about three years before we both said, "I promise to love, honor, cherish, and protect, Deloris/ Charles forsaking all others and holding only unto Deloris/Charles."

I would repeat those vows and marry Charles all over again. The reasons I fell in love with him are his caring and gregarious spirit, zeal for life, love of family, and faithfulness. After our engagement in 1970, he visited my home in SC on numerous occasions and during this time he showed love and kindness to me and my parents. My mother enjoyed cooking delicious meals for him, especially smothered chicken and rice, and my father enjoyed their long conversations about life issues. Charles was very friendly and he has never met a stranger. In fact, my father said that during the short time Charles visited Marion, he knew more people in Marion than him. He loved people in all walks of life. I enjoyed his talkativeness and knew that I wanted to spend my life with him. I especially enjoyed Charles' humor—at our wedding reception, he lifted my wedding gown up in a sneaky and coy way in order to reveal my garter. The manner in which he did it was so funny that it 'cracked me up.' He was continuously doing funny things like that throughout our married life. He was indeed a joy to be around. He said that he came to Marion, which is a small town, and got me out of the miry clay. We fell in love with each other.

After getting married, I moved to Durham where the two of us began our married life. He graduated from NCC and continued his professional career at IBM and I continued my career as a teacher. He was determined that he was going to move up the ranks in the company so that he could have a successful career and provide for his family. Also, he encouraged me to achieve greater social and academic pursuits.

Our family began to grow with the birth of our first child in July 1973. It was a blessing and joy to bring this little one into the world who was a part of the two of us. Charles was so very, very proud of our beautiful little girl – Sonya Deloris. The next year, we were blessed with a son— Charles II—and I thought this time for sure his chest would burst over with joy and pride. He was a caring father and tried to give Sonya and Charles II guidance during their formative years. He made frequent visits to their elementary school and directed their community athletic activities. Charles was very active in the life of Sonya and Charles II, but he and I were thrice trilled and overjoyed when Jennifer Bradley, our miracle baby, was born May 1983. He adored all of his children and was always telling people about their accomplishments. If he were alive today, he would be very proud of them. Unfortunately, my soul mate, my best friend, the love of my life died of a heart attack in July 1995. It was a very sad day in my life. Behind closed doors the tears flowed and flowed down my face as I remembered my loss and my family's loss. We had been married 24 years when he died and I had looked forward to us rededicating our vows the next year for our 25th anniversary. There is a saying: love begins with a smile, grows with a kiss and ends with tears. I have many fond memories of my late husband; of the love and life we shared together. The tears of missing him are a small price to pay for the many years of love and friendship that we shared. Yes, I would do it all again.

Deloris Harris

Robert and Taren Washington

I Lost My Friend and Love - Robert Washington

Robert Washington and Taren Claiborne married September 19, 1981

The loss of a loved one!

It was November of 1977 in a Films Art class at Evander Childs High School in the Bronx, New York when I first laid eyes on him. Handsome, articulate, and academically talented were the characteristics that made him so appealing. I decided to invite Robert to a sweet sixteen birthday party. Robert accepted the invitation and spent the evening dancing and dialoguing with me about many interesting things. Realizing that we shared a common bond, the friendship developed into a committed relationship. On September 19, 1981, Robert and I exchanged vows. This enduring marriage, built on a solid underlying friendship, with love, and devotion, survived many obstacles. The next twenty-three years of our lives was dedicated to building a strong and solid marriage.

I married my friend, lover, and confidant - a man who made my life complete. Working collaboratively, we embarked on new challenges while enjoying the riches of life, traveling and building a loving family with our four daughters Taren, Melissa, Morgan, & Meagan. In January 2002, Robert was diagnosed with leukemia which devastated the family. The value and importance of life was now viewed from a different perspective. Cherishing each day to the fullest, the Washington family enjoyed each other's endless love. The next two years were filled with challenges; endless nights spent by Robert's bedside praying and reminiscing about the wonderful times spent together with family and friends. On July 25, 2004, Robert succumbed to his illness, leaving the family distraught. At the age of 42, I was faced with the reality of being a widow and the sole guardian of our four children. It was my faith in God and the love for my children that gave me the strength and desire to live. As each day passes, the void in my heart is less painful; however, the yearning to touch and caress my husband remains. It's that special song, the unique smell, and the keepsakes that bring tears to my eyes. I pray every night for strength and thank God everyday for the union I shared with this special man, my friend, lover, husband, and great father! He was a pillar of strength, support and discipline; attributes that were instilled in our children. Robert is dearly missed and will never be forgotten. I would love to have the opportunity to marry him again.

Taren Washington

Taren Washington and daughters

"I married my friend, lover, and confidante - a man who made my life complete."

- Taren C. Washington

Henry and Sarah Jones

A Good and Giving Man - Henry T. Jones

Henry T. Jones and Sarah Claudia Scott married June 28, 1953

We met in Bridgeport, Connecticut during September of 1952. While I was standing at a bus stop with my friend Anne waiting to catch the bus home, Henry drove up and asked us if he could give a ride to wherever we were going. I said I was not getting in the car with a stranger. My friend Anne insisted, "There are two of us and only one of him, how harmful could he be?" Henry assured us he had no ill intentions and he would get us home safely because he wanted to take me out on a date. He said in order to do so as a gentleman he needed to know where I lived.

Henry was the first and only man I ever dated. Our first date was at the movies. After the movies he took me to meet his family and especially his oldest sister, Jessie. She helped him relocate to Connecticut to secure employment. He also told me that evening that he had two children from a previous relationship. This gave me a sense that I could trust him because he was straight forward and honest.

As we began to date regularly I noticed he was a good man with a kind heart and giving spirit who loved everyone. Henry never knew a stranger and didn't have an enemy in the world, unless you crossed him. One of his strongest qualities, that at times would frustrate me, was his willingness to care for others.

Our dating was a nine month whirlwind and included movies, ball games, trips to the park, New York City and meeting each others' family and friends. These activities resulted in our getting married on June 28, 1953. Who would have thought a girl from Georgia and a boy from South Carolina would meet and marry in Connecticut?

Our union resulted in us having eight children together (five boys and three girls) and with his two children we had a total family unit of ten (six boys and four girls). He was a great father to our children and one hardworking man. He would leave the house at 6 AM every weekday return home around 5 PM, and still made time to do activities with our children. During the Christmas season he would take a second job just to make sure we could get each of our children that special toy they requested.

Oh how he loved his children and family. As a treat on Fridays he would bring fish and chips home for the family. Saturday evenings we loaded all the children into the station wagon and took them to the drive-in movie. What we didn't have financially we had in love, caring, sharing and doing for each other and others.

Henry was a good and giving man - sometimes to the point I would get angry with him. For example, one month one of our neighbors was going to be evicted from their apartment if the rent wasn't paid in full so of course Henry paid the family's rent. This resulted in our rent being late that month and us incurring a late fee. He told me not to worry or be upset because that family had an immediate need and he considered having to pay our rent late (with a late fee) a small sacrifice to keep a family from becoming homeless.

My husband loved me but he also was non apologetic about being jealous and was very possessive of me. He affectionately called me his Sa (short for Sarah) - that was his name for me.

My husband died July 25, 2010 after seven years of battling Alzheimer's disease. It was difficult for me to see this once vibrant, big, strong, generous, caring, sharing, giving and loving man succumb to this cruel disease. I never thought I would have to visit him during our "Golden Years" in a health care facility but I had no other options. Neither I nor any of our children could give him the care (the Lord knows we tried to keep him home). This sickness required a high level of care. Even after he lost his ability to speak, he would still look at me and smile or nod his head to acknowledge my presence.

I miss him. I miss our conversations, his corny jokes, and his ability to cook some of the best tasting meals (despite leaving the kitchen in a total mess). I miss seeing the smile on his face when one of our children or grandchildren made him proud.

We had fifty-seven years together, I am happy he lived long enough to see our forty-eight grandchildren and forty-eight great grandchildren. Yes, I would marry him again if given the opportunity.

Sarah C. Jones

George and Barbara Bellinger

The Incurable Romantic – George Bellinger

George Bellinger and Barbara Prestwidge married October 7,1987.

I have been a widow for more than 7 years. Every day I remember something my husband George said or did that brings back the pain of missing him. In thinking about whether I would marry him again, the short answer is a resounding YES. The longer answer about why I would marry him again has to do with who George was as a person.

Certainly George was not perfect. In many ways he was a typical male. He would never stop to ask for directions—that was maddening. He sometimes left the toilet seat up—that was annoying. He made me a baseball widow all summer and into the fall—that was frustrating. And his engineering mind would lead him to solve some problems functionally while forgetting some nuances that needed to be considered simultaneously. Sending him to the grocery store was like opening Forest Gump's box of chocolates. I never knew what he was going to bring home—the brand, the amount, or how much he paid for it.

But I would marry George again because he loved me unconditionally and would do almost anything in his power to make me happy. He was happiest just being present and spending time with me. As a business owner and community leader participating on many boards of directors, he was very busy, but he had no trouble putting many things on hold when my needs or family needs required his attention. He made the time to be there when I needed him.

I would marry George again also because he loved my two daughters from a previous marriage and developed relationships with them that they cherish to this day. They still talk about George's opinions on various topics, what he would do, the funny things he would say and the things he taught them. Our lively dinner conversations, birthday celebrations, and holiday meals for Thanksgiving and Christmas are among their most cherished memories. They remember our vacations in St. Thomas and Cape Cod in the summer, leaf peeping excursions in fall, and trips to California to see the Rose Parade, to name a few.

Family was important to George and the many photo albums with hundreds of photos he took of our experiences together remain a wonderful gift and testament to our rich family life.

Another reason I would marry George again was because he was an incurable romantic. He liked holding hands and dancing with me. He actually courted me in a number of ways, and without being ostentatious or loud. For example, he sent me a card to ask me out on our first date. This was so weird to me at the time that it took my girlfriend to get me to stop, think and really appreciate his style. When we married, we shared a dream honeymoon for three weeks in London, Paris and Nice. During the whole time we were married George sent flowers to me for my birthday, Valentine's Day and Mother's Day. When I was having a tough day at work, he sometimes sent a card of encouragement or made appetizers carefully arranged on a decorative platter and had them waiting for me when I arrived home.

George did unusual, creative things like sending a messenger dressed in tails to my job on my birthday to deliver my birthday gift: lunch on a dome-covered silver tray. The messenger stood at attention outside my office door while I ate the lunch (a salad and a Diet Coke) and removed the tray when I was done. One year he took me and the girls to a mansion in Rhode Island for a Christmas dinner celebration, where we stepped in to the year 1812 upon entering the front door. Was this guy from Mars or what?

He was a positive thinker, who could always find a way to address an issue. For him, the glass was always half full. When I was diagnosed with breast cancer, he continually reminded me that I would overcome it, that surgery was going to be successful, and that I had many years to live. He was there when they rolled me into the operating room, and he was the first face I saw when I awakened in the recovery room. With his strong belief in the power of positive thinking, education and making a plan to achieve a goal, he was always ready to help anyone with an issue or problem. He did this for me, my girls, other children and families, and community organizations where he was a board member.

Finally, George had a great sense of humor. He told wonderful, funny stories of his childhood and other life experiences. That sense of humor often helped me relax and have a good time in the moment. Concerns became smaller, confidence became larger, and laughing with him helped me to remember to not "sweat the small stuff."

My married life with George ended with his death a few years ago, but I can say that our time together was wonderful, full of love, romance, laughter and shared family experiences that I will remember forever. For all these reasons I would marry him again.

Barbara Prestwidge-Bellinger

**Robert Herman Jackson and
Desretta McAllister-Harper**

A Man of Quality
- Robert Herman (Stonewall) Jackson

Robert Herman Jackson and Desretta McAllister-Harper married June 18, 1991

In the fall of 1968 Herman began teaching and coaching at North Carolina Central University (NCCU), and I began teaching in 1973. Although I am an avid football fan and went to every home and most away games, I never saw him until the fall of 1984 when one of my friends and a former student of his introduced us in the dining hall. After a brief conversation he asked for my business card. I expected that to be the end of the story, however two weeks later he called and asked if he could come over. That was the beginning of a twenty-six year friendship and whirlwind love affair.

When he arrived we talked for five hours. The next morning he had a 6:00am practice so he asked if he could come back the next evening. He came over every day for a year (provided that we were both in town). At Christmas, he took me home to Pennsylvania to meet his family and I took him to meet my family. Thankfully, there were no red flags from either side! In August 1985 he took me on our first vacation for a week to Curacao, Dutch West Indies. His children and grand children visited with us often. We travelled together sharing our love for football, both near (to Greensboro for North Carolina A&T State University Homecoming), and far (to the Meadowlands for New York Football Giants home games with Wellington Mara). After dating for six years there were so many qualities that stood out to me: his free giving spirit, intellect, honesty, spirituality, lifelong love of learning, regard for his appearance, sense of humor, sexual and artistic passion, and his core values. To top it all off, he made me laugh! All the above qualities were very important to me and made me know this is the man with whom I would like to spend the rest of my life.

When we weren't touring, we'd attend church on weekends, and during the week I watched him read his Daily Word and The Holy Bible. My teaching job caused me to travel frequently, but whether I was teaching in Jamaica or around the United States, he visited often. One of the summers I taught at the University of Missouri at Columbia, he came out to drive back to Durham, NC with me. He was also my personal trainer and masseur. When we met I had begun purchasing art. He admired my pieces and we began gifting artwork for special occasions like birthdays, Valentine's Day to each other.

I would marry him again, because he proved over the years all the qualities I saw in the beginning were truly who he was and he did not change on me. We were not afraid to say what was on our minds and when there was a disagreement we agreed there was one "fool" at a time. Our chemistry and commitment to each other never wavered.

He was a retired ~~military officer~~ educator + coach and by the time I retired we were both content to spend quiet days together at home. I only wish we could have gone on one more adventure together—living on a beautiful beach in some exotic location. However, we made the best of our time together. More importantly, I loved him for all those qualities that were important in 1991 and would marry him again in a flash today.

Desretta McAllister Harper

To my dear friend Tania
des 2-20-11

"I would marry him again because he proved over the years all the qualities I saw in the beginning was truly who he was."

- Desretta McAllister Harper

Isaiah and Laura Sneed

A Very Hard Worker and Proud Man - Isaiah Sneed

Isaiah Sneed married Laura Louise Cheek on December 15, 1943

My late husband Isaiah and I were married for 65 years, 6 months and 10 days. We dated for more than a year before getting married. I married him because he was kind and loving. We also had a lot in common: we both grew up on farms and loved to attend church.

Isaiah was a very hard worker. Although we didn't have much materially, he was very proud. He helped build our first home. We also owned a small farm. Although it barely had enough tobacco to make a living, he always had a large garden and an orchard. I worked with him and we canned, preserved or dried enough food to feed our family. Through our joint effort, we always had plenty to give away. Early in our marriage when I was sick, he had the patience of Job. He farmed, assisted with the children and took care of me. These years really brought out the commitment on both of our parts to our marriage.

Some of the happiest times during our marriage involved our four children—one son, Richard Isaiah, and three daughters Juanita, Gwendolyn and Charlena. Each of their births was special knowing that together, our love had brought forth new life. We both wanted our children to be educated so he insisted on borrowing money or whatever it took to make it happen. When they graduated from high school and college, Isaiah was full of pride—although, being from his generation, he didn't say it.

Throughout our marriage, the things that we shared the longest were our church and faith activities. He was a deacon for over forty years and I was equally involved. We also both loved to travel and attend family reunions—Isaiah even enjoyed them more than I did. We also made sure to never involve our children in any of our disagreements. We had plenty of them—65 years means there's a lot to talk about—but the children will tell you that they never heard us argue.

Isaiah was sick for five years and I waited on him for almost four of those years. When I became ill with congestive heart failure, my family insisted that he be put in a nursing home. This broke our hearts, but now we both had to be cared for. Our son and daughter-in-law moved in to assist me with everyday living, and he entered a nursing home near two of our daughters. Although we promised we would not put each other in a nursing home, he understood that there was just no other way. Since he passed, I miss him a lot and think about him every day. Sixty-five years is a long time and I never dreamed that I would out live him and be alone. Yes, I would marry him again.

By Laura L. Cheek Sneed

"Early in our marriage when I was sick he had the patience of Job. He farmed, assisted with the children and took care of me."

- Laura Sneed

"Our relationship can be compared to that of an "old shoe" - it fits just right."

- Vivian Williams

Solid

One In A Million

Terry and Vivian Williams

The Right Fit - Terry Williams

Terry Williams and Vivian Artis married July 4, 1975

We met on the campus of Virginia State University during Freshman Orientation. He was trying to strike up a conversation with my best friend but I interceded. The rest, as they say, is history. We've been married for over three decades and I would most certainly marry him again.

I believe that the true measure of a man is how he treats and takes care of his family. Terry is a great father, son, and husband. As an only child, I have been amazed at how he has cared for his mother through the years—including relocating her from New York to Virginia after his father passed in 2000. Our adult sons (Travis and Brandon) are his (our) pride and joy. I've seen him literally move mountains to ensure their needs are met. The love that we have for each other has blossomed through the years. We were very young when we married, but we have persevered and it has only gotten better with age. Terry and I are complete personality opposites but we complement each other perfectly. He's quiet and subdued, while I'm quite outspoken. He's not a "joiner," but I'm a community activist/public servant.

Our relationship can be compared to that of an "old shoe" - it fits just right. I can truly say that we both have honored the vows that we took: for better or worse, for richer or poorer. We have been and will continue to be there for each other. YES, I would marry him again!!!!

By Vivian Williams

Derrick and Shannon Steward

The Comforter - Derrick Steward

Derrick Steward and Shannon McLeod married August 30, 1996

I married my best friend. I know it sounds like a cliché but it is true. Derrick and I were friends for two years before we decided to become a couple. When we met 16 years ago, we both were divorced and were seeing other people. Although there was initial attraction, there was also the respect of each other's current situation. It wasn't long after each of our relationships failed we decided to date. I was quite reluctant at first, since I knew the kind of individual he is: although he's a hard worker, sweet and very respectful, he can also be stubborn and egotistical. One might say that these aren't the most engaging qualities of a man and a number of my friends would agree; but I saw an inner quality that to this day, I wouldn't trade in for the world.

As with any relationship, everyone has a past and my husband is no different. With several issues, including a failed first marriage, and an array of fiscal matters, any woman would more than likely run away, and initially the thought crossed my mind. "What in the world am I doing?" I would ask myself. I cannot begin to explain the number of conversations I had with close family and friends about pursuing a courtship with him fully aware of his situation. I received a lot of advice but in the end, I took it up to the Lord in prayer. I felt and continue to feel that the Lord does not make mistakes and he obviously put us together for a reason. I wouldn't say Derrick was my knight in shining armor, he was more like the comforter in a bad storm.

When I am with Derrick, I feel protected. It is as if the world could come crashing in all around me but I know that I am safe because he is there. Despite his setbacks, he not only allowed me to see his weaknesses, he also wasn't ashamed to admit them. That's difficult for any man to do, especially a black man. In addition to supporting me when I returned to school to earn my Masters and Masters Business Administration, he accepted my imperfections, and more importantly my daughter. He practically raised her and along with our son, I believe we have one solid unit. Now I can't say we don't have taxing periods from time to time – what marriage doesn't? Through faith, prayer and a lot of patience, we get through them.

To date, I would marry him again. The success of our marriage and our commitment to each other still shock a number of naysayers, and to them I say thank you. We thrive on the haters because we just turn that negative energy into something positive, fueling us more to reach the next level. We may have a long way to go before we reach our highest plateau but please note, I am truly blessed and grateful to have an awesome partner along for the ride. Derrick, let's continue to reach for the sky and love each other.

By Shannon McLeod-Steward

Steward Family

"I wouldn't say he is my knight in shining armor,
he is more like the comforter in a bad storm"

- Shannon McLeod-Steward

David and Darlene Deberry

My Selfless High School Sweetheart - David Deberry

Darlene and David Deberry Married October 19, 1991

We were high school sweethearts and dated for seven years prior to getting married. I married David because he has been my constant friend through thick and thin. When I met him I was a teenager with a very troubled home life. He never judged my family or my circumstances, but instead provided me with encouragement and a positive influence. I married him because he proved to be the quiet force in my life that affirmed me when no one else would. It also became evident after a few years of dating that we were indeed good together and good for each other. Together we created momentum—a sustainable balance of love, respect and passion—that resulted in us each living at our best.

I would marry him again because he is my confidant, lover and best friend. He is the foundation for our family and he is the love of my life. My life with David continues to exceed all of my expectations. I am not saying that we have not had our ups and downs, but what amazes me is the resiliency of our bond. I believe through our union, I experience the love of God every day. My husband is patient, he is kind, he is supportive, he is loving, and he is a constant companion. He is my protector, he supports my dreams and together we have created a life abounding in love, joy, and happiness. His most endearing quality is his selflessness, and from his life I have become a better person.

When we first got married I had just started graduate school. We had an infant son as well. David was the only one working, and he was also going to school. After a few weeks of school, it became apparent that our lives had entered into an unsustainable, tornado-like frenzy. I remember coming home from school late one evening feeling bad because I had left my baby and I was not contributing financially to the household. David must have sensed my internal struggle as he sat me down that night and said to me, "Listen, we are both working really hard. You are in school and taking care of the baby most of the day, while I am working, going to school and then rushing home to relieve you of the baby so you can get homework done. I will take myself out of school until you finish your degree, and then in two years I'll go back." At the time I had a full educational scholarship that I would have easily walked away from if he had asked. Instead he provided me with momentum. With his love and support, my husband pushed me higher. He took one for the team. This was a tremendous act of love. I have been careful never to under appreciate the magnitude of what it did for me personally and professionally. His selflessness exemplified for me unconditional love. It taught me the true meaning of sacrifice and vision, and made me want to work hard and finish successfully so he could have an opportunity to pursue his dreams.

I would marry him again in a heartbeat. The rhythm of my heart beats in melodious harmony next to his. In fact, my heart still does summersaults when he comes home from work because I remember the day when he gave so much of himself to me so that we could be more as family.

By Darlene Deberry

Deberry Children

*"With his love and support my husband pushed
me higher. He took one for the team."*

- Darlene Deberry

Kenneth and Lori Gibbs

The Rock - Kenneth D. Gibbs

Kenneth D. Gibbs and Lori Scott Jones married August 1, 1980

Kenneth (Kenny) Demire Gibbs, my husband of 30 years, epitomizes what a son, husband and father should be. He is God-fearing, loves and respects his mother and wife, disciplines our children and is always there for our family. He often tells me that I am the glue for our family. Well if I'm the glue he is the sturdy, firm and strong ROCK. In other words he is the foundation upon which our marriage and family is built.

I first met Kenny while in high school. We both attended an Upward Bound Summer Program at the University of Bridgeport in our hometown of Bridgeport, Connecticut. At that time Kenny was like any other guy to me—just a guy. You see, I was a tomboy and didn't have time for the guys at this time in my life. I do recall that Kenny was always a kind and soft-spoken gentleman.

Fast forward to New Year's Eve 1978. I had graduated college, returned home and my cousin Sylvia and I decided to host a New Year's Eve Party. I invited Kenny's good friend Ricky and I told him to invite any of his friends that maybe in town for the holidays. You might have guessed it—Ricky invited Kenny and another friend Aaron to the party. It was there that I noticed how handsome and dapper Kenny looked. He approached me said hello and we danced. I thought to myself, "Kenny is looking good, just finished college, unattached and with a whole lot of potential!" As we talked, to my dismay, he told me that he really enjoyed North Carolina and was returning there in hopes of securing employment. So to me there was no need for me to think about dating him since he wasn't going to be in Connecticut, where I was living at the time.

It was in the summer of 1979 that Kenny returned to Bridgeport, Connecticut and I ran into him again while I was doing a voter registration drive. The gentleman he was (and still is) he approached me and said hello. I acknowledged him and continued with the task at hand of registering voters. Unbeknownst to Kenny, I ran into his friend Ricky and I informed him I had just seen Kenny. It was then that Ricky informed me that Kenny was back in Bridgeport long term and seeking employment. In retrospect I realize I was rather coy because once Ricky informed me that Kenny was in town to stay, I made it a point before that evening to be in his presence. Conversation ensued and within two weeks, we went on our first date. Our first date consisted of us taking our two younger brothers to the Danbury State Fair. When Kenny dropped my brother and me off, he came into my parents' home where my mother and several of my aunts were sitting in the den at the time. My beloved Aunt Edna proclaimed once Kenny left "He's going to be Lori's husband!" Kenny and I became boyfriend and girlfriend in September 1979. We were officially engaged in February 1980 and became Mr. and Mrs. Gibbs, August 2, 1980… whew! I found out later from my now father in-law that I was the first young lady Kenny had ever brought to his parents' home and so he knew his son really wanted to marry me.

Kenny is a provider, protector and always there for our families. As a father, our children couldn't have a better dad. All three have grown to become adults and they each have a unique and loving relationship with their dad. To our daughters, he has demonstrated to them what characteristics to look for in a mate, husband and not to settle for just any male that wear pants. To our son, he has taught him how to be a man of character, who must uphold the family name with pride, dignity, honor and to respect women.

Kenny is a family man and we have become stronger as a couple as we have had to navigate through the trials and tribulations of life. He has treated my family as his own. As for our extended family, he has supported me and been there as we have allowed (usually at my suggestion) many of our nieces, nephews and friends to live with us in an effort to help them secure employment, strive to complete high school and/or college.

Marrying Kenny and becoming his wife is the best personal decision I made in life. He is the calm to my excitement. He is the patience to my impatience. He is the quiet to my storm. He is the rational to my irrational. He is the practical to my radical. He is strong when I am the weak. He is the silly when I'm too serious. He is my caregiver when I'm sick. He makes me laugh/smile when I'm sad and he is my lover. He loves me and shows his love for me.

I love him and I'm in love with him. I salute him and I'm proud to be his wife and yes, I would marry him again—for all the reasons listed above, and many, many more!

Lori Jones Gibbs

Gibbs Children

"Marrying him and becoming his wife is the best personal decision I made in life."

- Lori Jones Gibbs

Here and Now

Camera Shy

Clear Vision – Timothy Earl Norris

Timothy Earl Norris and Miriam Thomas married –January 1, 1983

I met Timothy Earl Norris of Philadelphia, PA in the spring of 1980. We were employed at the same time in the NBC affiliate in Fort Meyers, Florida and were the only African-American employees at the time. As such, I recall my boss "encouraging" me to meet and greet the new guy, who was coming in from Philadelphia. Someone from the TV station had gotten Tim all settled into his local motel room, when I went bouncing over there with a bottle of wine and a warm welcome – only to encounter the shyest guy I'd ever seen in all my 24 years! I remember thinking "this guy is 'weird' shy"—to the point of hiding his face behind the magazine he'd been reading when I knocked on the door of his room! Not much conversation ensued. I remember thinking, "This guy ain't my type at all!" I soon left, saying to myself, "Welcome to Florida, buddy. You're on your own!"

A few weeks later, we were actually speaking to each other on cordial terms. He seemed like a nice enough guy (and was, as it turned out) – but still, struck me as kind of weird. He was *so* shy. All he did was ride his bike and play basketball—and I never liked jocks. Long story short, all of us at WBBH were so young (and so broke) that we all ended up sharing apartments (except me—I didn't have a roommate). Tim soon moved in with another fellow employee, but when that guy got a job somewhere on the East Coast of Florida, Tim needed a new roommate. By that time, a loft apartment I coveted had become available in my complex, but I could not afford without a roommate. So I soon offered to let him move in with me! By the way, this was an arrangement I carefully kept secret from my parents in Alabama over the ensuing months because there was no way they would approve of me having even a nice young man sharing my loft! I was apparently fooling nobody. I still laugh at the memory of how my folks soon figured it all out and how my Dad had a habit thereafter of occasionally asking, "How's your bunk buddy?" (LOL!)

A couple of years passed, and when I received the "dream job" (at the time) offer to move to Durham, NC and anchor the weekend newscast at WTVD-TV, I promptly left Tim to fend for himself! To my surprise, he saved up and bought me a beautiful one quarter-carat engagement ring (a yellow diamond!) and drove to NC to present it to me! What happened next is still a palpably painful memory for us old married folk, so I will give it short shrift. During Tim's visit to Durham, that ring was accidentally flushed down the friggin' toilet and never seen again! We overcame that misery, eventually married on New Year's Day of 1983, and went on to parent two beautiful children, a son, Ryan Montgomery, and two and a half years later, a daughter, Nicole Yvette. Our children are now young adults of whom we are extremely proud! Ryan and his wife Natalie (nee Natalie Moore, of Connecticut) met as students at North Carolina Central University have since given us a grandson and still live in Durham, NC. Nikki is currently a senior at Winston-Salem State University.

The rest of the story is really fairly short and sweet. For all of these years since, (we were married 28 years on New Years Day, 2011) Tim has been the most wonderfully sweet, gentle, warm and amazing husband and father I could wish for. He has supported me on countless occasions during a very challenging and most difficult (although rewarding) 20-plus year professional career in television news, when family and children often had to come second to the news of the day. And perhaps most importantly, Tim has proven over the years to be a better parent to our two children than I could ever hope to be, including various stints as PTA President, and being the best cook in the family! He is truly the man!   I would most assuredly, absolutely marry him all over again!

Miriam Thomas Norris

The Southern Gentleman - William Edward Bolling

William Edward Bolling married Mary Elizabeth Roy August 1, 1953

I met William through his sisters who were my friends at the time. You see, I went to his three sisters' home so we could eat prior to going to the movies together. His sister told me to go in the kitchen and turn the fried chicken. This man entered the kitchen and asked "Are you my sisters' friend or did you come here to see me?" I looked at him like he was crazy and told him no, I was not there to see him and his sisters and I were going to the movies. He replied, "I'll take you to the movies, but if I do, you have see what I want to see little girl". You see I was 18 years old at the time and he was a 30 year old man.

My mother loved Edward from the start because he was a true southern gentleman. He always came to the house, brought flowers and other gifts not only for me but my mother as well. We dated for two years. Later we married when I was the ripe old age of 20 and he was 32. There were no children of our union.

It was during our two years of dating that I came to realize that Edward had a jealous streak. He had little tolerance for men he thought were "competition" for my time and attention, which in essence was any man that was not my father or brother. An example is a male friend I had grown up with and was like a brother to me. One afternoon Edward saw me sitting in the car talking with this man, and boy did he let me know he did not like it—insisting that I not do it again. Edward could fuss enough that he could chew the color out of rag—he was my quiet storm.

My beloved Edward died in 1989. Sometimes I find myself thinking I need to tell Edward this and that. However, I realize I can't tell Edward anything, because he is no longer here on earth with me. However, his spirit is still strong and so is my love for him. I still miss him and I long for the sound of his voice, the touch of his hands and the fabulous dinners he prepared for us. I remember, the conversations we shared and the love and commitment we had for each other. Yes,

I would marry him again. Edward loved, protected and provided for me. He was a good husband, always nice to me. He was a sharp dresser who possessed character, strength and the willingness to help others by sharing of his time, talents and treasurers.

Mary Elizabeth Bolling

"I would marry him again because he is the most wonderful, sweet, gentle, warm and amazing husband I could wish for."

- Miriam Thomas Norris

The Three C's of Marriage - Keys to The Marriage Covenant

Communication, Companionship and Compatibility

"*I would definitely marry him again. It is my prayer that our girls will grow up and share their lives with someone just like their "Daddy".*"

- *Kara Vample Turner*

This book project started as a tribute of African-American wives to their husbands. Along the way, as I would describe this project, some sisters dealing with marital strain would say to me, "I wish I could write something like that about my husband…we've just drifted apart over the years." Younger sisters, who are still looking for love, would ask me things that they might look for in deciding whether or not to marry a man. All would ask me what do I attribute the success of my marriage to and I would respond with the three C's - Communication, Companionship and Compatability.

Keys to the Marriage Covenant

Marriage is above all a covenant between three parities: man, woman and most importantly, the Lord. As is written in Matthew 19:4-6:

"Haven't you read," he replied, "that at the beginning the Creator 'made them male and female,' and said, 'For this reason a man will leave his father and mother and be united to his wife, and the two will become one flesh'? So they are no longer two, but one. Therefore what God has joined together, let man not separate."

Since it is God who joins us together in matrimony, His instructions are the ones that we must follow in order to have a successful marriage. Today marriage is generally thought of strictly as a legal contract. In legal contracts, each party tries to maintain their personal interests and get as much as they can out of the other while offering as little of themselves as possible. However, the covenant of marriage involves following God's leading as you love your spouse, above all others, at all times, sacrificially and selflessly. This is why we state the vows we do in our ceremonies: "forsaking all others, for better or for worse, for richer or for poorer, in sickness and in health, for richer or for poorer, to love and to cherish, till death us do part."

In order for a marriage to work, there has to be commitment between the partners. Below are a couple of practical tips—the three "C's"—that make a marriage work.

Communication: Let's Talk

When the musical group The Moments sang, "I Found Love On A Two Way Street…and Lost It On A Lonely Highway," they must have known that in order for a marriage to succeed communication is key and that it's a two-way street. Communication does not mean simply talking to each other. More importantly, communication means listening to each other. Hear the words your partner is speaking and listen for what it is s/he is saying to you. True communication is open, honest and tempered. As it says in Colossians 4:6 "Let your conversation be always full of grace." Think about it. You, more than anyone else on the earth, know what words to say or buttons to push to make your spouse happy, confident, energetic or upset, depressed and without confidence.   Use this knowledge to build up your partner and your relationship, not tear them down. We would all do well to follow the instruction found in James 1:19-20:

"Everyone should be quick to listen, slow to speak and slow to become angry, for man's anger does not bring about the righteous life that God desires."

Too often, we are slow to listen to our spouse, quick to speak and even quicker to become angry when we feel s/he is not "understanding what I'm saying." However, this only results in hurt feelings, and shutting down of further communication.

When couples are not communicating their marriage is at risk. Sometimes this results from arguments. However, sometimes the busyness of life means you no longer prioritize time to check in on your spouse. Instead of loving him/her above all others, as you stated in your vows, your partner and their needs get pushed to the back burner. Now I understand from experience that there are a host of "real life" responsibilities that come up and that can limit the time that couples have to communicate with each other. They include family (children, parents, extended relatives), work responsibilities, money matters, and community activities. However, you vowed to love your spouse "above all others," so communication with him/her must take precedent over everything else. I will expound on children, work responsibilities and money matters in this section.

When it comes to children, remember it was your love, verbal and physical communication with each other that helped you create the bundle(s) of joy. Too often, the demands of those bundle(s) of joy end up limiting your communication with each other. If anything children should increase your communication, especially when making decisions about them. I am firm believer that parents—whether married or not—must mutually agree to have a consistent and unified voice when communicating about and to their children. My husband and I always decided that any disagreement about the children would happen behind closed doors—in our bedroom. Then, once we made a decision, we came out as a unified force and communicated our joint decision to them. We encouraged our children to have a voice, and express their opinions. However, ultimately the final say rested with us: we were their parents and so we make the final decisions of our household.

Work responsibilities are a part of life and all responsible adults want to provide for their children. However, as we became an increasingly two-income earner society, we have stopped communicating with each other and lost focus on family. Nowadays many families no longer sit down and have breakfast or dinner together, go for a walk together or simply check in with how each other are doing. The race to have the biggest & newest house, car or gadget, and to over indulge our children has created additional demands on our time. These demands limit our time together, and reduce time for communication, putting a strain on our marriages.

Since the start of our marriage, my husband and I both have worked outside the home. However, by God's grace, we also made sure that all of our decisions were for the betterment of our family. This meant, we both realized we could have it all, we just couldn't each have it all at the same time. With that said, we mutually agreed and communicated that one of us would be the primary care giver and the other the primary breadwinner. So, for the first 20 years of our marriage, my husband got a steady, high-paying job as a corporate tax accountant, and I got off the career "fast track." Instead, I worked in institutions that allowed me to continue to grow and contribute professionally, while allowing me the flexibility to take time off to attend all of our children's events and to take care of them when they were sick.   Once the children left for college and we were empty nesters, I took a job in corporate America and my husband was able to pursue his dream of opening his own accounting practice. He had taken care of the family financially for the first twenty years of our marriage—dutifully providing for a family of five—and it was now my turn to financially take care of just the two of us. Again, I stress that this only worked in our relationship because we were unified in the goal from the start, and continued to communicate with each other every day to ensure that each other's needs were being met.

Communication is also key when dealing with matters of money. Money can be a very contentious issue for couples, especially when they view money differently. Often times, this results in one partner shying away from conversations dealing with money. Trust me, not talking about money, finances, credit and investments can lead to a house with no foundation. Often times when I am speaking with women about money matters they say, "His money is *our* money, but my money is *my* money." While this is an interesting perspective, is it right to expect him to bring all his money to the household and for you to hold back a few dollars for yourself? As the scripture says, *"They are no longer two, but one."* This applies in all areas of marriage, including money. I can do an entire book on this topic but instead I will cover a few areas on the importance of communicating about money and some practical tips to make those conversations as smooth as possible.

- Your attitude about money and money matters probably come from the behavior you observed in your parents about money. Therefore, you should take some time to evaluate your own attitudes about money and then communicate with your partner. Be true to yourself and your attitude about money. For example, are you a spender or a saver?   You know the answer. If, for example, you are a spender, do not think that just because you've fallen in love and gotten married this learned behavior will instantly change. More likely than not, you will continue to spend. The only problem is you are no longer a "me", you're now part of a "we" and have another person to consider.

- Remember that "the love of money is the root of all kinds of evil" (1 Timothy 6:10, NIV). Do not make the common mistake of putting your value for money above your value for your spouse. You and your spouse can do a number of things to minimize the all-to-common fussing-and-fighting about money and prevent the strain these issues can bring into your marriage:

    ○ Write out a detailed budget. For example, how much money is brought into the household each month (your combined "take home pay" before any expenditures), and what are expenditures you have each month (mortgage/ rent, car note, insurance, groceries, childcare, utilities, cable, credit cards). Make sure you include **everything**.

    ○ Identify which expenses are essentials versus those that are "nice to haves" but that you can live without. Then, establish common goals and work to achieve them together. Decide who will be responsible for paying the bills and whether or not you should have separate checking accounts for the essentials (such as household expenses) versus other things (like entertainment).

    ○ Live below your means. Just because you all make a certain income does not mean that you need to spend every dollar you make. Do not try to "keep up with the Joneses." From my twenty-five years in the financial sector, I can tell you that more often than not, the Joneses are fronting and have their own money/financial troubles.

    ○ Pay for your needs, plan (save) for your wants, and know the difference. For example, gentlemen, you may need a dependable car. However, that doesn't mean that you need a Mercedes Benz or Lexus. Ladies, you may need a pocketbook, however that does not mean that you need a Gucci. Let me give you a tip from a friend of mine who says, "If the pocket book costs more than the amount of cash money you can keep in it on a regular basis you can't afford it." Therefore I say put the Gucci pocketbook back, leave it at the store and wait for the sale. Remember, you probably already have several pocketbooks in your closest that you no longer carry, but nothing's wrong with them. In time of financial strain, knowing the difference between a "need" and a "want" can make all the difference in keeping peace in your marriage.

Following the suggestions above will help bring a financial unity into your marriage. As you make progress toward achieving your financial goals, you will feel empowered.   Finally, remember no one likes to talk about money, but it is necessary. You are a team so it's important to keep open communication so you can enjoy working towards your common money/financial goals of freedom and security.

Companionship: In Other Words I Got Your Back

God said, "It is not good that a man should be alone" (Genesis 2:18) – this statement equally applies to women. Eve was created as a companion for Adam. The husband is "the companion of her youth" (Proverbs 2:17, NKJV) and the wife is "your companion and your wife by covenant" (Malachi 2:14, NKJV). It is therefore safe to say that true love and marriage is more than just a partnership—it is companionship.

A marriage filled with companionship will lead to a lifetime together. When you are asked the question, "Who is your best friend?" you should easily respond "My spouse!"

So what is companionship? Companionship is defined as, "association as companions, working together, fellowship, camaraderie, friendship."

Companionship is important in a marriage and comes by working at being your spouse's best friend. This includes learning to share goals and interests, supporting each other, focusing on long-term goals, being prepared and ready to work for a successful marriage and taking time to romance and date your mate. You'll notice the words "working" and "learning" in the above sentence. This is because the best and most genuine companionship comes from years of getting to know and understand your partner. I once heard a minister say that couples should at least date through the four seasons of a year because as the seasons change, this will give the couple time to get know each other prior to leaping into marriage.

One example from my own marriage of knowing and learning to share the other's goals and interests comes from our recreational activities. My husband loves (let me repeat, loves) playing tennis for both socialization and exercise. Although I was OK with tennis, it isn't at the top of my list of activities to select. However, because he loves it, I support him in by once in a while going to watch him play. This makes him happy, he smiles at me as I sit in the stands and after he finishes playing he comes over, gives me a kiss on the cheek and tells me thanks for coming. I, on the other hand, enjoy doing community service activities through my sorority. This work often requires that I travel. I have learned how to bring my husband with me on some of my trips to places I know we will both enjoy ourselves. I call my sorority sisters and find out if their husbands (who are also coming on the trips) play tennis, or know how to put my husband in touch with the local USTA tennis team. We are both happy doing what we like and the trips give us an opportunity to talk and communicate with each other, romance each other and spend quality time together.

Anything in life that you really want and that really is worth having requires work. You have to prepare for it and to work to keep it. This is how people approach their education and their careers. Know that marriage is no exception to this rule. Therefore in order to keep your sacred bond to each other you must work through the storms, earthly temptations, struggles, and challenges (both mental and physical). Some situations will be more challenging then others. However, by following God's leading and working together, you will get through it all. Remember, when you got married you committed to each other for better or for worse. It will be your perseverance and determination through those "worse" times that will make your marriage work, and will get you to a happier, calmer and more peaceful marriage.

Remember the long-term goal is having a happy, successful and enduring marriage.

Compatibility: Let's Agree to Disagree Sometimes

Marriage is a union where two people in love have committed to spend the rest of their lives together. Many people will go into marriage thinking it's a never-ending honeymoon, the truth of the matter is a marriage is having the ability and the willingness to overcome difficulties, agree to disagree and learn from past mistakes. However, it becomes challenging when issues continually arise and compromise is almost impossible. The truth is many allow love and romance to be the determining factor for a marriage. Yes, you must have both for a marriage to work. But soon, as the newness and excitement ends and reality sets in, the question you both must ask before getting married is "Are we compatible?"

You probably heard the elders say marry your own? I often wondered what that meant. Did it mean marry within your race, religion, financial stratus, personality type, and/or educational equivalent? Or did it mean to marry someone you are compatible with? Compatibility is a must, yet it is something that many relationships lack.

You've seen them on television or heard about them on the radio. There's Match.com, e-Harmony, Christian Singles, Black Singles and the list goes on and on. These companies know what the elders knew, people are looking for love and compatibility. These companies have used science to develop compatibility quizzes and personal profiles to help their clients find their life mate. While researching the above mentioned websites they all asked questions that fall into the following compatibility categories:

- **Communication (Let's Talk About It)**: Are you direct or indirect? Are one of you an extrovert and the other an introvert? Is one of you a talker? Is one of you the silent type?

- **Personality (Yours and Mine)**: Do you really get along, or find that you are silently irritated with the other person's personality? Are you uptight and your date is laid back? Do not go into a marriage thinking you're going to change your mate—that would be a mistake. If your mate was a jerk when you met and dated, he will bring that same personality into your marriage.   Personality is a very important factor, and the most difficult to change.

- **Financial (Money Matters)**: Money matters!! Are you a spender? Are you generous or frugal with your money? How is your partner with their finances? Money is one of the things couples fight about most often. It helps (but is not absolutely necessary) if you have similar financial goals and means.

- **Family and Friends (Yours, Mine and Ours)**: When you marry your mate, their family and friends come along, as do yours. Ask yourself if you get along with each other's family and friends. Decide how you will make decisions regarding each other's family and friends. Family and friends can be a source of stress for your relationship. Remember that your marriage is primarily about the two of you, and it will survive them as long as you and your mate jointly agree on how to handle family and friends.

- **Health and Nutrition (Fitness It's A Lifestyle)**: Are you a health food nut or a junk food junkie? Is the only exercise you get channel surfing? Look at if your health-related lifestyles match or not.

- **Educational (Pomp and Circumstance):** Some studies have found people tend to feel the most comfortable with others who share similar life experiences, professional opportunities, and world views.

- **Intimacy (Let's Get it On):** Romance, intimacy and closeness come into play here. You may love to cuddle in public while your mate may prefer private affection. Your mate may enjoy foreplay before sex and you may want to go straight to the main course. If you're not fulfilling each other's intimate needs, your marriage is at risk of one or both of you going outside the marriage to have those needs met. This will probably lead you to divorce court. However, don't despair if your initial intimate forays are less than fully satisfying. Talk to each other about what turns you on and listen to your mate's needs. With enough work to accommodate each other's intimate needs, you will be able to rock each other's world.

Finally, marry your best friend. This is the individual who you plan to spend the rest of your life with. Marriage partners should know each other inside and out: their wants, needs, interest, goals, fears, and desires. Couples that rush into marriage and do not value the friendship aspect may find themselves consulting with others about their confidential marriage issues. This lack of friendship may also lead to infidelity.

Friendships that evolve into relationships result in relationships that are lasting. The individuals have already established a bond and have come to know each other. This is good because we tend to show our friends who we really are, more quickly than we would someone pursuing us. Our friends see our weaknesses and faults, as well as our strengths and virtues. Friends know our background and the reason we may behave a certain way.

Compatibility will never be perfect. We are all imperfect and have faults. Some of these faults we see early and others not until later. The couple that is truly compatible and has developed a friendship will deal with problems accordingly. The love must be strong enough to endure and the good must outweigh the bad. This results in a strong, solid marriage foundation.

All the marriages profiled in this book embrace the Three C's (Communication, Companionship and Compatibility) of marriage and all have weathered the trials and tribulations of life. With love and commitment to and for each other, their marriages are strong and lasting. To God be the glory.

"I would marry him again because he is known as Dr. Love...he loves his God, his wife, his sons and family"

- Judith Davis

Tips That Help Make Marriage Work

Tips that help make marriage work and keep the flame burning:

Marry your friend, the man with whom you have things in common.

Understand that there's no competition in a marriage.

Don't marry him if you think you're going to change him.

Be ready to be married. Marriage is not a romantic comedy its real life.

Marry a man who is honorable, loves you unconditionally, cherishes you and respects you.

Depend on him and reinforce his masculinity. Remember he's a man and wears the pants, but you zipped them for him. No man intentionally leaves his home with his pants unzipped.

Leave work and your work armor at work! He knows you're the strong, confident, self-assured woman at work but he wants his soft and caring wife at home.

Men need attention so make time for him. Date him and make him your central and only focus for a certain period of time at least once a week.

Let him think he's right, even if he's wrong. He'll realize the errors of his ways and the make-up will be worth it.

Let him watch all his sports and sports channel. It gives you the choice of joining him, reading a book or going to another room in the house and turning on Lifetime, OWN or any television channel for women.

Be happy he loves and respects his mother. His mother is not your competition. She'll bake him a birthday cake but he will enjoy your "cake" more.

Always give him your "cake" when he asked for it, that includes when you're not in mood. Man by nature is a lover of sex.

Remember they're his children too. You may have birthed them but he gave you the seed to help create them.

Let him cry he has feelings too.

Let him know you love him. He needs to hear it, see it and feel it.

Never go to bed angry with each other. Stay up late and work it out if you have to. In the end kiss, make up and move on together.

Resources for Black Marriage:

African American Healthy Marriage Initiative
www.aahmi.net

Black Marriage Publications
www.blackmarriage.org/Black_Marriage_Publications/Welcome.html

Wedded Bliss
www.weddedblissinc.com/Wedded_Bliss_Foundation/Welcome.html

Black Marriage Day
www.blackmarriageday.com/Black_Marriage_Day/Welcome.html

The Urban Institute Making Marriage Work
www.urban.org/toolkit/issues/marriage.cfm

"I would marry him again because I discovered that he is the one and he had always been the one."

- Glenda Gabriel

Salute Your Husband

Salute Your Husband

Photo of the two you

Your Written Salute To Your Husband

About The Author

Lori Jones Gibbs is a Vice President with a major financial services company.

A graduate of the University of Connecticut, Ms. Jones Gibbs holds a Masters degree from the University of Bridgeport.

She is the co-author of the book *Yes, You're Approved! The Real Deal About Getting A Mortgage and Buying A Home* and the forthcoming book *Yes, You Can Have More Money Than Month.*

She is a member of Delta Sigma Theta Sorority, Incorporated and First Calvary Baptist Church, Durham, NC.

Jones Gibbs is married and has three adult children.